Play Sport!

By Sally Cowan

Sport is fun to play,
and it gets kids fit.

When kids play sport,
it is good for them.

Kick!

You can try many sorts of sports.

You can skip with a rope.

Jump!

You can go for a bike ride.

But do not ride in a storm!

It's not safe.

It's fun to speed by
on two big wheels.

But honk your horn to tell others
you are there!

Honk!

When kids play sport,
they can play for a team.

The kids do drills to get
more skills.

You might score!

Kick!

Golf is a great sport for kids.

This coach shows the kids
the right form to hold
a golf club.

First, look for the flag.

Then, aim for the hole and **tap**!

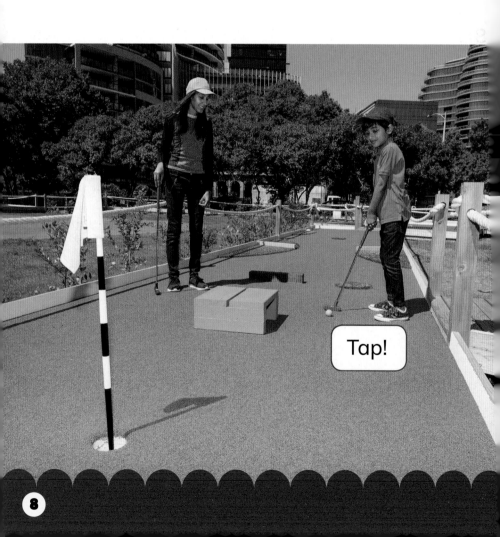

Tap!

ots of kids like to run on a track.

You can run if you are short or tall!

Run!

But first, reach out your legs.

Then you will not get sore
when you run.

You can do sport inside, too.

Jump in for a swim and
kick your legs!

You can ride a horse
as a sport, too.

Neigh!

Kids can play all sorts
of sports!

They can skip, ride and kick,
or tap, run and swim.

Which sports do you like best?

CHECKING FOR MEANING

1. Why shouldn't you go for a bike ride in a storm? *(Literal)*

2. Why should you stretch before you run? *(Literal)*

3. Which of the sports in the book do you think is the most difficult? Why? *(Inferential)*

EXTENDING VOCABULARY

fun	What other words could you use instead of *fun* to describe something you like doing?
horn	What is the meaning of the word *horn* in the book? What else can it mean?
form	What does the author mean by *the right form to hold a golf club*? Why do you think *form* is important in golf? What else do you need the right form for?

MOVING BEYOND THE TEXT

1. What are some sports that you can play indoors?

2. Which sports would you rather watch than play? Why?

3. Do you prefer team sports or individual sports? Why?

4. Why are sports such a popular pastime?

SPEED SOUNDS

| ar | er | ir | ur | or |

PRACTICE WORDS

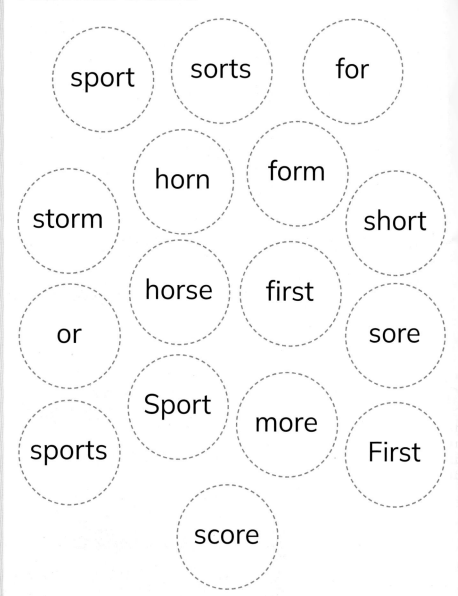

sport

sorts

for

horn

form

storm

short

horse

first

or

sore

Sport

more

sports

First

score